MIDDLE-CLASS EMPLOYEE WANTING MORE? RISE AT 5AM TO CHANGE YOUR LIFE.

LONGING FOR FREEDOM AND HAPPINESS IN YOUR LIFE? WANT TO KICK OUT STRESS AND ANXIETY?

RUSSEL JACOBS

CONTENTS

As a **Thank You** for getting my book, included with your purchase, is a checklist on "**7 Signs You will Soon start Feeling Disgusted with your Life, and How to stop it from Happening**".

I thought you might like it.

Click on the link below to access it.

The Seven Indicators

INTRODUCTION

It was on March 1, 2010.

What happened, you ask? Good question. It's the day every-thing changed for me. My then boss, whom I will call Mike, walked to my cubicle at 9:17 am, sat down on a chair right beside me, looked me in the eye and said,

"Russel, I just want to let you know we might be downsizing in the next couple of months.........".

Was I eventually laid off? That's a story for another time.

What's important is, at that moment, I knew I had to take more control of my circumstances in life by trying to be as indispens-able as possible and have an exit strategy.

You might also be having these worries about the uncertainties of the future, but you're hopeful. However, you also know you can and should take steps to shape the future and even your current circumstances. It's is entirely up to you. What you do today and continue doing tomorrow and the day after will determine the quality of life you lead tomorrow.

You know you work hard and that you always have.

You might not be facing a lay off as I had a couple of years back. But maybe you've been in the same job for many many years, and, while happy enough, you know you're capable of so much more.

The COVID19 pandemic might have also made you realize that your highly secured job you loved so much, well, is not as secured as you might have thought it was.

You want to be free. Free to decide what to do with your time and not worry much about paying the bills and providing for your loved ones.

Maybe you might have figured out that you need to start a business, exercise a little more to be healthy, and get more in touch with yourself for inner peace, but you have not just found the time to do so.

You might have even carved time out in the early morning or late evening hours to do some self-development, but it only lasted for a few days.

You might have even figured out you could wake up early in the morning to start taking control of your life but have little or no clue what to do next.

Maybe you're a shift worker, trying to figure out how to get more out of life. You know for a fact waking up early has some fantastic benefits, but wondering how you can benefit from it because you are very much awake already at that time. Not very much by choice though :).

Because of either of these concerns, your stress and anxiety levels go through the roof.

The moment comes for most of us at some point in our lives, in which we look at ourselves in the mirror and say, "I want more."

"I want to be free." "I need to figure this out sooner than later."

When I had that moment, I knew I needed to make changes in my life to make my dreams real. So, I made the changes, and it worked.

I shared what I'd discovered with friends, family, relatives, and co-workers. It wasn't before long that everyone asked how I did it, so I started writing about it.

When I tell people that rising at 5 am is the key to their dreams, I'll sometimes get a blank look. People don't like the sound of rising at 5 am. It's just so – early.

Yes. It is. And in those early morning hours, is the fruit of life you keep reaching for, never quite able to grasp it. Waking up earlier has allowed me to change my life by pursuing the dreams I'd never had time for.

In this book, I will explain how I went from being "happy enough" with life to being "ecstatic" with this simple plan for living well, and to your fullest potential.

The best part is that you only need to follow the plan 5 days a week to get what you need from the practice. And once you get used to this routine, you'll wonder how you lived without it!

So, read on friend, and unveil how to be happier, healthier, more productive, stress-free, anxiety-free, and successful by becoming the luminous morning person you didn't know you could be.

1

THE BEST VERSION OF YOU

You're an extraordinary person. I know that because you're reading this book, hoping to find a formula to get you where you want to be in life.

So, this book is here to help you become the best possible version of you. Already a going concern, you're looking for just the right kind of push to make your dreams a reality. You're hard-working, successful, but you want more.

You're like my friend, Karl. Karl is an extraordinary guy who's always the first person at the office and always the last to leave. Karl has learned that life doesn't always bring you the opportunities you desire. He's learned that sometimes you need to go the extra mile to get what you're after.

But now, Karl has hit a bit of a brick wall. He's a leader in his company but feels there's nowhere else to go. Happily married and raising two kids, he's ready to make his next move. He wants to feel healthier and happier, but he also wants to find that magical next step forward. He just needs a plan to make it happen. If that sounds like you, you've come to the right place. Rising at 5 am may sound like a bridge too far. You may be a faithful night owl, or maybe you just don't like the sound of the hour. Maybe you're in love with your snooze bar!

But what you need to know is that 5 am is a bridge to something spectacular. You're not just getting up early for its own sake. You're getting up early to achieve something.

So, let's talk about this idea. Some don't necessarily agree that 5 am is all it's cracked up to be. Let's look at some of the more common objections to the practice before reviewing the benefits.

Not everyone's a morning person.

True enough. I wasn't for many years.

But the truth is that many people don't like rising at 5 am because they tend to stay up later than they should – we'll talk more about that later.

Science separates people into two groups when it comes to rising early in the morning. Larks tend to get drowsy earlier in the evening, whereas owls like to stay up late.

But mostly, human sleep cycles are governed by circadian rhythms controlled by the brain. When we sleep, the suprachiasmatic nucleus, which consists of 20,000 neurons, regulates our hormones and runs our digestive system. In all these cases, we're talking about natural rhythms in the body.

Part of this can be blamed on genetics, but we can manipulate the circadian rhythm by approaching the challenge with diligence and consistency.

Just remember that about 47% of your sleep preferences – early vs. late – are established by genetics. That's a hill to climb, certainly. That doesn't mean you shouldn't put on your hiking boots.

You need that sleep!

This was my favorite excuse for not getting up early. But how much sleep do you really need? Let's look at the numbers.

You're an adult, so you don't require more than 8 hours of sleep each night. As a matter of fact, adults function well on between 7 and 9 hours of sleep. We've all been that teenager who sleeps until 11 am. But teenagers do require more sleep – marginally. They need between 8 and 10 hours, according to the National Sleep Foundation.

And sure, we all need to sleep, but what's your attitude towards rising from bed? Are you hitting the snooze bar repeatedly, then finally dragging yourself out of bed less than half an hour before you need to be at work? That's called a "habit." That's got nothing to do with whether you're a lark or an owl and every-thing to do with what you've become accustomed to doing in the morning.

But it may well have plenty to do with your evening routines. If you're having difficulty getting out of the bed in the morning, maybe you're probably not getting to bed early enough. More on this later.

You've convinced yourself of something which is not true – that you can't get up at 5 am because you're not wired to do so. You're a night owl.

Not that there's anything wrong with being a night owl. But you should know that it's the larks that get that worm. Larks get up early and enjoy better cognitive functions during daylight hours than night owls do, and who doesn't want that? You? I don't think so.

Even night owls can change their ways, so let's look at some of the benefits of rising at 5 am and why you need to do it!

You will be blown away.

There's something about the early morning that has captured human beings' imaginations since the time humanity began to record their thoughts. But I think Benjamin Franklin said it best when he said, "The early morning has gold in its mouth."

Most of us have experienced the magic of darkness, giving way to dawn. We've all stayed awake through the night, completing homework or other projects, or perhaps, unable to sleep. We've got up early to catch flights or go on long road trips. The early morning has a magic all its own.

How would you describe that magic?

I'd describe it as the gentle, satisfying knowledge that you're awake while the rest of the world seems to be asleep. The quiet is almost a presence. The morning traffic and ambient noise have yet to ramp up. The world around you is serene, peaceful.

How often in your busy life do you feel that way? How often do you have the sensation that you're alone in the world for a moment, listening to the velvet silence before dawn breaks? The tranquility of the early morning hours holds in it a deep sense of promise. And we don't get to experience that very often these days.

Imagine rising at 5 am, 5 days a week, and enjoying that tranquility every working day. Before entering the world's noise and brashness outside, this is your own time. This is when you work on yourself, your plans, and your dreams. In that is a timeless wellspring of self-nurture that should be cherished.

And here's the thing you need to know – you can't argue with science. Well, some do ;). Science says that the peaceful early morning is extremely beneficial to your overall health for the following reasons:

- Your brain enjoys the benefit of increased oxygen levels in the blood.
- Blood pressure is reduced.
- Those who suffer from migraines have fewer of these when they rise early.
- Your mental health is strengthened.

Our 21st Century lives move at the speed of light, rarely allowing us to catch our breath, much less reflect. Instead, we react to the changing conditions around us. We're always looking out for the next priority - the next bullet point in an endless litany of todos.

Dr. Fatima Ali is a psychiatrist who also points to technology as a roadblock to our ability to step into tranquility and be nourished by it. The constant presence of screens in our lives has made it difficult to allow our brains to rest and rejuvenate. Rising at 5 am gives us the kind of quality time our brains need to be at their best. Slowing down and embracing the morning peace allows us to add a reflective component to our frenzied, hyperactive lives.

The Journal of General Psychology, in 2008, published a study that affirmed the value of rising early. Those who did so significantly enjoyed enhanced productivity. At least some of that productivity boost though, is connected to the discipline of establishing set times to both sleep and rise. Getting the right amount of sleep must be factored into an early-rising routine, or it's not going to do you much good.

In fact, not getting to bed at a pre-determined hour can lead to depression if you're also rising at 5 am. Sleep is essential to your ability to function effectively, so getting in those hours the night before, is where the whole project starts.

Recalibrating your circadian rhythm demands that you be consistent and diligent about going to bed at a time that allows you to get the sleep you need. Your day doesn't really begin at 5 am – it begins the night before, at the sleep time you've set for yourself.

5 am – What are you going to do with your time?

The alarm sounds, and you're out of bed in a heartbeat. You're ready to start your new life as an early riser.

So, what are you going to do with all those lovely morning hours? While that's up to you, I have a structure I believe you'll like. But first, let's talk about what rising at 5 am means.

- Rising at 5 am means you have an extra 2 hours minimum, to work on your life goals, your pet projects, and yourself. And if you're going to get up at 5 am, then you know you need to make those 2 hours count.
- If you start work at 8:30 or 9 am, you have a three and

a half to four-hour window. Factor-in the time you need to shower, eat breakfast, and get to work and adjust accordingly.

- We've established that you need at least 7 hours of sleep each night to be at your very best, so schedule your bedtime for no later than 10 pm. I know. That's going to take some getting used to, but you can do it, and I'm here to make it easier.

- When you get up at 5 am, you're giving yourself 2 full hours to accomplish your goals. How will you do that? You will make those 2 hours count, setting them aside to correspond with a precise morning routine, which is accomplished before you leave to get to your day job.

PREPARING FOR A GOOD NIGHT'S SLEEP

We've all had those nights. Those nights when, no matter what we do, we can't get to sleep. If difficultly falling asleep is one of your roadblocks to rising at 5 am, there are a few changes you can make to render falling asleep much easier.

As I've pointed out in this book, the 21st Century is noisy. It's also very illuminated. 24/7 light is a way of life for us in a security-conscious world. So, two of your challenges are going to be noise and light pollution.

Street and neighbor noise are realities for most of us, especially if we live in cities. Your best bet to eliminate this problem is to invest in some noise-canceling earplugs. Spend a little bit of money. Sleep in peace.

Another strategy for noise is the use of white noise machines or tapes which play soothing sounds like the waves breaking on a beach or wind rushing through the trees. It all depends on what you feel comfortable with. I will not insult your intelligence by directing you to links online (amazon, etc.), where you can buy these items at very affordable prices.

Electric light is your second challenge. Many find it difficult to sleep at night due to this factor. The streetlights, the neighbor's porch light, or car headlights – all these can make falling asleep difficult.

My solution? Blackout curtains. These are available almost everywhere these days, as electric light is such a problem for those trying to get a good night's sleep. Lining your drapes with a heavy fabric is also a fantastic solution. Remember that the denser the weave of the fabric, the more light it cancels.

The modern world can interrupt our sleep because of Trojan Horses like the blue light emitted by mobile devices, notebooks, laptops, and computers. I advise you to limit the use of these devices, to areas of your home outside the bedroom. Simply, the light emitted by electronics screens interrupts melatonin production (the hormone that helps you sleep). Because of its shorter wavelength, blue light can seriously interrupt your sleep cycle.

I also recommend moving the television from your bedroom. The bed is for sleep. It's not for doing your taxes, eating a sandwich, or catching up on your emails. Respect the place you sleep by eliminating sources of sleep disruption and deprivation, including the television. But if you can't get it out of that room, then make sure it's turned off at 8 pm (2 hours before you need to go to sleep to rise at 5 am).

If you're going to sleep well, you need to plan for that to happen, and you need to help your melatonin do its job – which is to help you sleep – by creating the right conditions. That means removing all blue light from the room you sleep in.

For some people, it may also mean relaxing in a hot bath before bedtime, or listening to soothing music, as you drift off – or a white noise machine. Sleep is such an individual thing, so find the strategy that works best for you.

Everything I mentioned above falls under the rubric of "setting the stage." You're going to be creating the conditions necessary for a good night's sleep, so you can start using your early mornings to go for the gold you know is out there.

In the next chapter, I'm going to move onto meatier matters – like your life's purpose. While that may sound lofty and a bit esoteric, I'm willing to bet you already have some idea about what that purpose is. Maybe you're reading this book because you're looking for a way to move closer toward it. But one thing's certain – those fresh, tranquil early morning hours will help you realize it.

You need those 7 hours. If you don't get them, you're working against yourself, your purpose, and your goals. You are sabotaging yourself. And while I know the television is a common source of relaxation for many, it's also what keeps many of us up after bedtime. It is a time-eater, so if you're having a problem with that aspect of your life, maybe limit your viewing, to accommodate the sustainability of your new wake-up routine.

So, as promised, let's take a deep dive into sleep and how you can make sure you get enough of it.

Rome wasn't built in a day.

Things that last take time to build, so don't rush yourself.

Suppose you're one of those who has a rough time getting up earlier than you're used to, start by rising 15 minutes earlier. Then, try a half-hour and then 45 minutes. Keep going until you've got your sleep cycle where you want it.

And you're going to need to move that alarm clock out of reach. Your snooze bar is no longer accessible.

Once you're awake, get out of Dodge. I mean – leave the room. Laying around, thinking about getting up, is not "awake." Once you're out of the room, you tend to start your day, so leave. Fast!

Remember, you get the weekends to cultivate your hobbies, love your family up, and do whatever else you love to do in your spare time. So, don't be sad! It's only 5 days a week!

GET THOSE 7 HOURS OF SLEEP

Adjusting your bedtime can be as tricky as adjusting the time you habitually rise. But getting these 2 things right is the key to rising at 5 am.

7 hours of sleep a night/day – because you're a shift worker – is the reasonable minimum you can expect to fully function on. Less sleep than that, and you run the risk of self-sabotage.

SLEEP CYCLES

The National Sleep Foundation states that most adults experience 5 or 6 sleep cycles, as they sleep. 5 of those cycles consume just over 7 hours. So, get that sleep. Uninterrupted sleep cycles help to maintain balance in your mind, as well as in your body. This is when your body repairs itself, and your brain rests – with the exception of dreams – the brain's method for resolving outstanding concerns.

If you find that you need more than 7 hours, try 7 and a half or even 8. There is a range of between 7 and 9 hours for adults between adolescence and the senior years, so experiment to discover what's "just right" for you.

THE MOST COMMON SLEEP CHALLENGES

Quality is always preferred over quantity, so set your sites on quality sleep. Following is a list of the most common reasons people have problems getting to sleep and staying asleep.

See if you recognize any of these challenges as your own:

- You are eating after 8 pm. If you eat well, you shouldn't need to eat anything after dinner. I know people do it, but eating at night is more of an entertainment than a necessity. It can cause digestive problems and nocturnal "calls of nature" that interrupt your sleep.
- Busy brain. Our brains are busy little beavers, and sometimes, they just won't quit – especially when we want to sleep. When this happens, try to distract yourself by focusing on sleep intention. For example, by repeating: "Now I will sleep." Or go into the Livingroom and read until you're drowsy. Take a warm bath. Do what it takes to get into "sleep mode."
- Room temperature. Too hot? Can't sleep. Too cold? Can't sleep. That said, a cooler room is better for sleep than an overheated room. Ventilation matters too, so crack a window or turn the fan/AC on and, if necessary, toss on a blanket.
- Blue light in your sleeping space inhibits melatonin production (which helps you sleep), so banish it. Don't

use your screens in the room you reserve for sleep. No phone. No laptop. No Kindle. No tablet.

- Electric light. As I said earlier, get the blackout curtains, or the curtain liners. Turn off the hallway light beaming into your bedroom. Darkness is what your brain and body need to fall asleep.

- Alcohol. Sure, it's a depressant, but if you come home after a few and roll into bed, you'll be awakened in the middle of the night as it wears off. Enjoy your liquor if you have to, on the weekend.

- Caffeine. A powerful stimulant, coffee should be consumed in the morning and never after 2 pm. We love it. We need it to roll out the door, but it can have you staring at the ceiling if you are not wise.

- Exercise. Engaging in activity that elevates your heart rate right before bedtime is another insomnia culprit. You've got your body all excited, and now you want it to rest? A tall order. Exercise should not be done less than 5 hours before bedtime.

- Sleep apnea. A problem for many people, this is an interruption in breathing. If you suffer from it, I suggest you talk to your doctor about a solution.

And remember to stick to your schedule. As I've explained earlier, habits are formed by being consistent over a period of time. When you're consistent for 21 days, the habit is formed. Be consistent. Form the habit.

And please, relinquish the idea that every problem has a solution in the form of a pill. Pharmaceutical sleep aids are not the answer. They can have long term health consequences. Even consuming melatonin supplements is inadvisable. The solutions are in you – not a pill.

I have something better! It's a technique used at the United States Navy Pre-Flight School, which trains pilots to fall asleep in 120 seconds. With this simple tool, you can do it, too. But know this – pilots in the training program usually take about 6 weeks to master this skill. But once you've got it, you've got it for good! This is how it's done:

- Lying down in bed, relax your face, including the muscles inside your mouth. This is where many of us hold our tension.
- Relax your shoulders, arms, and finally, your hands. Don't move down the arm until the shoulders are relaxed. Don't move down to the hand until the arms are relaxed.
- Take a deep breath. Exhale slowly as you relax your chest and mid-section.
- Relax your thighs, then the lower legs, then the feet. You should be feeling a little droopy at this point in the exercise.
- Visualize something you find relaxing for 10 seconds.
- If you're not yet in the land of nod, say the words, "don't think" for a further 10 seconds.

- In the space of those 10 seconds, you should be asleep.

You have a bit of a hill to climb, but it's not insurmountable. In fact, I'm willing to bet you're already thinking about your own techniques for falling asleep more quickly and perhaps, adjusting some habits to make sleep come more readily.

We're all human, with challenges, including the fear of change. But the changes described in this book are what you can do to move your life to the next level. And you know that's well worth the admission price since you've read this far, right?

What the morning routine can do for you is endless. It disciplines you. It nurtures you. It encourages you, and it empowers you. Those 2 little hours give you the time you need to lean in and get where you know you should be, as a high-achieving and ambitious, middle-class employee.

The middle class is the backbone of our nation, so when you help yourself achieve your dreams, you're helping others. You can bet that your circle of friends, family, and colleagues will want to know what's come over you. What has changed about you, and how did you do it? Trust me; they'll ask because it will be written all over you.

Imagine getting your life wrangled into the shape you want it to be. You are the maker and shaper of your life, and that's why you know that you must prepare yourself to achieve that shape.

It doesn't matter if you're a shift worker or a 9-to-5 middle-class worker. What matters is that you know that small changes can make a tremendous difference. And while getting up earlier isn't that small a change, I can assure you that it's not that big a change either. If I can do it – and I was a night owl most of my life – you can too.

And I know you will because you've read this far.

Let's take a look at shift workers and how they make the morning routine work with their schedule!

JUST FOR YOU SHIFT WORKERS

This section is just for you guys! If you're a shift worker, you may well be working at 5 am for all I know.

But 5 am can happen any time of the day, depending on your schedule. The concept is to get your 7 hours of sleep in and rise 2 hours earlier than usual. If you're working shifts, you can do it at any time.

Is your challenge to find the quiet space you need for your wake-up routine – see? I even changed the description for you.

So, just to keep you focused on the question, here are the time allocations for the recommended wake-up routine, again:

1. Visualization, Affirmations & Thanksgiving (VAT): 12 minutes

2. Mindfulness Meditation: 30 minutes
3. Exercise: 18 minutes
4. Work on your goals in order of priority: 36 minutes
5. Review: 24 minutes

Let's say your shift ends at 11 pm. Your commute home takes about an hour. You get in bed at about 12:30 am and rise at 8:00 am. You would have two hours to go through your wake-up routine from 8 am to 10 am.

In our second shift work example, let's say your shift ends at 7 am. We'll assume an hour to travel home. So, you get to bed at 8:30 am and wake up at 4:00 pm. You'd be conducting your wake-up routine until 6 pm.

But as I noted, I don't know what your shift is like. My point is that you can adjust this any way you choose, by building in the wind downtime after work, or other life necessities. The goal is to get that wake-up routine attended to.

Change is difficult for most of us, but I know what shift workers are dealing with. And it seems there are a lot of you out there. The US Bureau of Labor Statistics says there are about 15 million shift workers. This includes people who work rotating shifts, evening, and night shifts. Your circadian rhythms are set upon, to begin with, so I know this will be challenging for you.

But change is always possible, no matter what your schedule is. You can adapt the advice in this book to slot into your unique work/life balance. And you will because you're going places!

2

A MARATHON – NOT A SPRINT

You're attempting to make a major life change that will benefit you in the future in ways you're not even fully aware of yet.

It's paramount that you adopt the mindset of the marathoner. This is not a sprint. This is a long-term, sustained effort toward realizing your most cherished goals. Anything in life worth having is worth expending the effort for, and rising at 5 am is no different.

But before you start, you need to reflect on why you're here, on this planet, and what you're here to do. A big deal huh? I know! But we all have a purpose and knowing what that is, will be a significant motivating force for the life change you're about to make.

So, where do you start? I'm sure as I write, you may already know what it is. The idea had perhaps languished in the back of your mind, for a variety of reasons. Sometimes people are afraid to ask what they really want in life, or they've listened to negative voices around them which say they can't do it or shouldn't do it.

But it's your life. It's your purpose. That's important enough for you to push aside any negativity you've encountered and any fear you're harboring about getting what you want and deserve from life.

Let's look at some ways to pinpoint your purpose, so you can start to focus on realizing it.

PUTTING YOUR FINGER ON YOUR PURPOSE

Many of us spend our whole lives thinking we must be missing something. We meander through our lives, asking, "Is that all there is?" But there is more, and it's up to you to put your finger on the purpose you may have been flirting with but not actively nurturing.

You need to center yourself in pursuit of that purpose. Let's start with some questions that will help.

1. What's your favorite flavor of broken glass, and do you eat it with or without a lemon slice?

No matter how much you try to avoid it, we all know that life can be difficult. There are good days and bad days.

But when you know your purpose, you can take the bad with the good, right? There's going to be "bad." It's inevitable. Finding your purpose isn't some silver bullet to a flawless, crimp-free life. It just doesn't work that way.

What you really need to ask yourself is what you're willing to do and what you'll happily sacrifice to get what you want from life.

The truth is, perfectionists, the languid, and those who fear failure are not getting anywhere. It's only the fully invested who eventually gets to where they want to be. So, eating your favorite flavor of broken glass - with or without that lemon slice - is what you sign up for. You sign up because this is what you were born to do, and you know it.

2. Imagine you're watching your adult self as an 8-year old. Are you crying yet?

What did your 8-year-old self, get lost in for hours doing? Maybe it was creating art or putting on impromptu performances. Maybe it was fiddling with machines or fixing bicycles.

Why did you stop?

It's a funny thing, but sometimes we stop doing the thing we love most because we're raised to believe we need to work at any job that comes along, whether we hate it or not – because that's what adults do.

But what would your 8-year-old self say about that? Probably nothing. Poor 8-year-old, you would probably just cry for the death of your passion.

Your passion is what makes you happy. It's what turns you on and lights you up. Your parents may have told you there wasn't enough money in whatever it was that made you happy, or that it wasn't a "good enough" thing to base a career on.

That kind of negativity can haul someone up short, kill their dreams, and chill their hope. Ignore it now, as you wonder if 8-year-you wasn't on to a good thing.

3. What are you doing when you're so focused you forget to eat?

Do you tend to drift off when you're doing a particular activity? For some, that might be writing or embroidery. It might be studying the mysteries of the universe or playing the piano.

Why do you think you're so fascinated with this activity? What are the primary skills required by this activity that demand your attention?

Examine the activity that causes you to forget about the world around you and ask yourself how it pushes you to activate specific ways of thinking that other activities don't. In that knowledge is a clue about your purpose.

4. If you had a choice, what would you be doing all day today?

The purpose is about action. You can't realize your life's purpose by sitting on the couch and staring at the TV or scrolling through other people's social feeds.

A purpose is just a dream without action. It just sits there in your head, as your life goes on – purpose-free.

Ask yourself these questions, but don't answer them unless you're ready, to be honest with yourself. Personal honesty and integrity are the foundation of figuring why you're here and what you're here to do.

EMBRACING THE JOURNEY

You're starting a journey toward your purpose. But you're already on a journey because you're alive. Moving intentionally toward your purpose just makes the journey more exciting and fruitful.

There will be a certain amount of discomfort on your journey – fatigue and failure are just two of the contingencies that may crop up. But discomfort is often what makes us address our "growing edges" – the part of us that needs a little extra tender loving care.

Adversity and discomfort tend to be considered negatives, and to a certain extent, they are. But the fruit of adversity and discomfort are growth, change, and learning.

Every failure, head on the desk moment, every frustration of your plans, is an opportunity to learn and grow as you journey through your purpose.

As you get closer, you'll see opportunities to lift the boats of others. This is one of the great rewards of having a life purpose – sharing what you've learned with others to improve their lives.

Your journey is highly personal; that much is so. But your journey is also a human triumph. You are intentionally creating the life you want by pursuing the purpose you're in the throes of visioning. And that's worth sharing with others who would benefit tremendously.

But how will I know it's right?

Your life's purpose is a big deal – maybe the biggest deal you've ever wrangled. But there's no need for anxiety. Your purpose will find its way to you because you're going to give it a little push in that direction.

And what's more, once you and purpose finally get together and start making waves, you'll know you're right and that your purpose is what you were born for.

We're all born with a deep sense of who we are. But somehow, as we grow into adulthood and take on all the associated responsibilities, something changes. We start to think more in terms of "making a living" than what we really want to spend our existence doing.

We lose the insistent inner voice that called to us before the age of reason silenced it.

Imagine, for a moment, the billions of people on this planet going to work every day, dragging themselves out of bed and plodding toward a daily working life they can't bear. That's no way to live, and that's why you're looking for something more fulfilling. You want to live an authentic life that honors the gifts and aptitudes you've had bestowed on you.

- What do you love?
- What comes to you like breathing?

What you love – the thing you return to repeatedly, fascinated, and obsessed by – is the key to the purpose. What is it? What makes you lose hours, as you pursue the subject or skill that makes you happy?

If what you love comes to you like breathing - effortlessly, then you're even closer than you were a minute ago. You have a natural affinity for the thing you love. It comes naturally because your innate gifts were tailor-made for it.

How do you wish to be perceived in the world?

What are two qualities you would love to be known and remembered for? These will point you toward sharing the love you have for your emerging purpose.

These qualities can be everything from confidence to joy. What is your meaning as a person living out your purpose out loud? What does it offer others?

Maybe you want to inspire people to find their own purpose. Or maybe you want to build a rocket and send it to the moon. Whatever your purpose is leading you towards, the perception of others is critical. What do you want most to share with them?

STATE YOUR PURPOSE

With all these things in mind – and I realize it's quite a bit – it's time to state your purpose!

Sit down and think about how different the world would be if all were going precisely as planned. Ask yourself what difference your purpose will make in the world.

Imagine people learning from your experience and living their best lives because of what you've done with your life's purpose. What does that look and feel like?

You may want to write something like, "Lifting others up by inspiring, teaching and sharing" or "Changing lives with the power of community." It all depends on what you've identified as your purpose and how you're going to deploy it to arrive at the life you want.

THE HEART OF THE MATTER

It's in your heart that your purpose first grows. The heart of a child, undeterred by negative opinions, knows what it's there to do.

Look inside yourself to pinpoint what your heart is telling you. You can read this book and many others, but your heart is your guidance system, expressly there to help you find your way.

All you need to know is where the journey begins and what its ultimate destination is. Your heart will tell you the rest. But it's the child's heart that will fill in the blanks on the way there.

The purpose is about action – goals help to facilitate the process.

You're getting a handle of your purpose, but how do you get there?

You get there via a progressive discipline of setting and then, realizing goals. Without goals, our lives are rudderless.

Setting and realizing goals is like having a touchstone – goals tell you where you are in terms of getting to your life's purpose.

So, let's talk about how to set goals and how long and short-term goals fit into the picture.

KEEP YOURSELF HONEST

How do you do that? How do you keep tabs on your time and how you're spending it?

How, a calendar of course, and today, there are so many options, both electronic and dead tree, so choose the method that works best for you. Every goal has action items, so make space for planning the realization of these items and timelines for their realization.

Your computer and mobile device have calendars, but maybe that's not your style. As I've said, anything from a Moleskin notebook to a sophisticated digital calendar may be just what you need to keep yourself honest.

And once you've gotten that in place, you're ready to set up your immediate and long-term goals and the action items that accompany them. Like a project manager, you're going to allot a completion date and benchmarks to that completion. As you strike each one-off, remember - you're getting closer to where you want to be.

And the purpose is what motivates you!

So, what do goals look like? Here's a short list to get you started:

- Clear
- Specific
- Measurable
- Positive
- Realistic
- Achievable
- Flexible
- Time-bound

You might be familiar with the goal-setting acronym-SMART. Any goal, genuinely worth its salt, is clear. You have stated, unequivocally, what you want to do. There is no ambiguity in goal setting. You have a goal, and to get it completed, you will be taking specific action steps to achieve that. And if you know exactly what your goal is because it leaves no room for misinterpretation, it's much easier to set the action items that will get you to completion.

It's a specific goal, for instance: "I will learn to code by 2022." It's not "Take a coding course." The coding course is an action item toward your goal to learn to code by 2022.

Because your goal is clear and specific, it's measurable. All shades of grey have been edited out. You can clearly see when the goal has been reached; there are no loose ends. Goal achieved!

And keep your goal setting focused on the positive. If you want to stop doing something, you can do that on your own time.

For example, quitting smoking is a lofty goal, but it's debatable as to its impact on your life's purpose (unless you're planning to build a smoking cessation aids empire, of course). Stay positive. It's in the positive that we find our best selves.

You may be huge fans of Elon Musk, but please don't write, "Build a rocket to the moon by 2030" as a goal unless you have access to the kind of revenue, talent, and infrastructure Mr. Musk enjoys. Be realistic. Know what's sustainable.

Realistic goal setting walks hand in hand with the achievability of your goals. You may have a dream of working in a foreign country, but you'll need to learn the language and culture, as well as get a work permit and legal permission to remain there. So, that may be a long-term goal, with the action items being your visa to live in the country, your work permit to work in that country, together with the requisite language skills, represents shorter-term goals.

An achievable goal is one you know you can reach in the time you've allotted yourself, so consider that as you set your goals.

Something important about goals that need to be remembered is that contingencies happen. In fact, life would be a little less exciting if there wasn't the odd disaster coming at us from time to time. We learn from contingencies. We adjust to them. Your goals may take a hit from unforeseen circumstances like COVID-19, illness in the family, a sudden change in living conditions, and any number of other blips that might show up on your radar.

Short-term goals help you reach for what you need right now in learning/skills development, which is a step towards realizing your purpose. They build momentum for long term goals. As I said above, to make your dream of moving to a foreign country, there are steps you must take. Your action items are short-term goals. As you achieve them, you move toward the long-term goal, and it becomes closer to realization.

Use that calendar. Use deadlines. Use all the tools you have at your disposal to create goals that won't make excuses!

YOU'RE AWAKE AT 5 AM! WHAT NOW?

And now, we're getting to the good stuff.

But before we do, here's an important health tip – before you eat anything, down a glass of water (8 ounces). Set another one next to you as you follow through your morning routine. Those 2 glasses of water are needed by every cell in your body, including your amazing brain, which will be much more efficient when hydrated. Your organs will be activated and hydrated after a night's sleep. Happy organs – happy early riser!

You're up, bright-eyed, bushy-tailed, well-hydrated - and you're ready to plan your precious morning time. If you're not as described, don't worry. This gets much easier, as your circadian rhythms adjust to the new normal.

Having 2 hours in the morning to complete the activities that will push you toward your life's purpose is what I recommend. It's a substantial slice of time, and once you're doing it, you'll wonder why you didn't start years ago. So, if you need an earlier wake-up time, by all means – get up earlier. But those 2 hours are going to become crucial to your success, so rock them!

In this chapter, I'll introduce you to the components of your early morning routine. We'll go into a lot more detail about these in the next chapter, but here, we'll introduce you to the essential components.

VISUALIZATIONS, AFFIRMATIONS, AND THANKSGIVING (IN ADVANCE)

This section of your morning routine may be new to you. You may not understand the purpose of these actions, but you will soon, and once you do, you'll embrace VAT, as the valuable set of tools it is.

Allow yourself 12 minutes for this section of your early morning plan. Some days, you may have to adjust the amount of time you have according to contingencies, so be prepared to be flexible, adjusting your time allotted according to how much time you have. For example, if you only have one hour instead of two, this activity should be allotted 6 minutes.

You may be new to the practice of visualization. But you need to know about it, and you need to practice it. Why?

Because if you can see yourself doing something, performing all the steps to achieve the result, you're visualizing, you can do it in the real world. Visualize yourself meeting your goals like a finely tuned machine, for starters! This powerful tool will change the way you think about yourself and your abilities.

MINDFULNESS MEDITATION

Like many folks these days, you probably grab every delicious extra minute of slack time you can. But then, you probably tend to oversleep and be rushed, running wild-eyed out the front door, juggling a coffee and an energy bar with your keys and maybe even your phone.

I knew a guy like that. He showed up one day wearing only one sock.

But he was the kind of guy who sat up all night watching TV, even though he had a 9-to-5 job. He said he needed it to relax.

Mindfulness meditation is a practice that centers you by slowing down your breathing and concurrently, your thoughts. Racing thoughts are stressful. What mindfulness meditation invites you to do is to walk away from that source of stress and focus on the moment.

Find a quiet spot in your home that you'll use every morning. Wear comfortable clothing and be aware of your breathing and posture. Lay down or sit up – it doesn't matter, so long as you're comfortable enough to breathe more deeply and intentionally. This portion of your morning requires 30 minutes. More on this later.

EXERCISE

You're a high achieving middle-class employee, so you could be any age from 18 to 80 – or more, these days!

So, I'm not about to assume anything about your state of physical fitness. What I am going to do is tell you the truth – regular exercise is the key to living a better life.

If you don't exercise at all, then it is urgent. You will thank me later. Just look for a form of exercise you enjoy, and that is sustainable. The bite-sized morning workout will wake your body up – including your brain, which will benefit from your highly-oxygenated blood.

You may not like it much at first, but as the days and weeks go by, you'll see and feel the fruits of your labor if you're consistent.

I include several exercises in the next chapter, which may appeal to you, as they need no equipment. So, no excuses! Devote 18 minutes of your morning to this component.

SPEND TIME WITH YOUR GOALS

You've been thinking about your goals and how to achieve them. As part of your morning routine, you're going to spend some time working toward them, so prioritize.

Long and short-term goals are addressed in this component. The clarity of the morning will allow you to crystalize your plans. You'll also be immersing yourself in the future you're building.

Books are a great way to reach at least some of your goals, especially if they're concerned with building skills or knowledge. Or maybe you'll read other books like this one, supporting you in finding the way forward. That's partly why this book is here – to point the way.

Do you have a blockbuster business idea but haven't had time to get a handle on it? Maybe you want to retire by the time you're 40, and this blockbuster idea is your plan for making that happen by doing it on the side.

Or maybe you need that promotion so bad for additional income or whatever your motivation may be; only you lack that certificate or skill, which is a core requirement for the position.

The time is now – during your 5 am morning routine.

That's important, so think about where it belongs on your list of goal priorities.

Combining the realization of short-term goals with long-term goals creates a picture of what you're building toward. You'll see how your short-term goals feed into realizing dreams that are set further in the future.

Remember that clarity is crucial when it comes to goals. If you've done an excellent job defining the steps you're planning to take, it'll be easier to prioritize them and then, achieve them. Take 36 minutes of your morning to work on your stepping-stones to success – your goals.

Time to review!

Again, this part of your morning routine is about goals. But you'll be looking through a different filter to assess them.

We all know that conditions can change – rapidly. We've certainly seen that proven by the COVID-19 pandemic. Robust businesses and supply chains all over the world have been hit hard.

Sudden changes in conditions demand that we plan for them, even when we have no idea what they may be. Did you see COVID coming? Probably Not. But when you're prepared for contingencies, you're better able to weather the storm.

And change demands our honesty. Now that you're building a matrix of long and short-term goals, you're coming to under-stand the path you're on. But you're also learning about how you see your place in the world – your life's purpose. You know that there is hardly a journey that goes in a straight line. There are going to be mountains and rivers and all manner of glitches along the way. That's why you need to be adaptable and resist the temptation to cling to a goal that needs to be adjusted to serve unforeseen contingencies.

There is no life skill more in demand than flexibility and adaptability. The leader who can deftly change direction is the leader people look to for answers. Apply that adaptability to your goals and watch the skill grow.

This goes for both short and long-term goals. Tomorrow, murder hornets or walking sharks might be the contingency – we know that anything can happen!

Learning to adjust your goals is learning to embrace change. The goal is still there, but events have changed the strategy. That's a challenge, and you are wired for challenges.

Some people never learn to embrace change. We fear it. We rail against it. But embracing change is where your growth edges are perfected, just like metal in fire. You will become stronger, faster, and smarter when you're able to pivot when change comes.

Now, you're coming to the end of your morning routine, so take a moment to plan your day. Are you addressing your goals effectively? Are they realistic and achievable under existing conditions?

You're engaging the day ahead by looking through your calendar. You are prepared for your day because you have deliberately and intentionally planned your actions. Dedicate 24 minutes to a realistic, honest review of your goals and a preview of the day ahead.

And you've already done so much! You can now calmly go about taking a shower, getting dressed, and calmly walking out the door and into the fantastic day you're about to

face with enthusiasm. We're going into much more detail about the components of the morning routine in the next chapter. Let's take a deep dive into what you'll be doing at 5 am!

3

YOUR MORNING ROUTINE IN-DEPTH

Now that you've been introduced to your 5 am morning routine, it's time to find out more about some of the components.

You might not be familiar with some of these activities, so I'm going to talk about their value and how you'll benefit from them.

Get to know your morning activities and how they feed into your future dreams and aspirations.

VAT (Visualization, Affirmations and giving Thanks in advance)

This component of your morning routine is how you'll "center" and prepare yourself for the coming day. This is self-care, and yes, everybody needs it, especially when working on creating the life they want. Nurturing yourself is part of what's required.

So, let's break down the VAT, one letter at a time, starting with the "V."

VISUALIZATION

"To bring anything into your life, imagine that it's already there."

— RICHARD BACH

Everything that human beings make is the result of an idea. When seen in the mind, in all its constituent parts, that idea is the result of visualizing the steps required to create it. Starting with the wheel, it's the human imagination that has created the world we know, inventing, perfecting, and progressing toward even greater, more effective solutions.

This is precisely what visualization intends to do: See it. Do it.

If you can picture yourself performing a task or creating something, you can perform or create it. Imagine that your mind has such power. But this is very real. What you can create in your mind is what you can create in the 3D world.

So, when you apply visualization to your goals, you're actively setting them in motion. There is a Greek word that expresses this process well, and that word is "praxis," which means "reflection leading to action." Praxis, then, is a two-part process, perfectly describing what visualization is.

At the heart of successful visualization, is intentionality. You and I both know that we already visualize but in a very casual way. We tend to immerse ourselves in the "what ifs." Maybe we have an important meeting, so we plan what we're going to say. We visualize ourselves at the meeting, ready with the right words.

These incidental visualizations aren't what we're talking about here. That's why intentionality – the deliberate act of visualizing the emotional effect on you, of a specific goal when realized, is so crucial to the process. There is a clear purpose.

Next, visualization requires a specific process.

That process involves visualizing the steps you'll need to take to reach the specific goal being focused on.

For example, you want to learn to code. You find the right class, then enroll. You attend the classes and start learning. You progress to the next level of coding, and finally, you're an advanced coder. You go and get that job you want.

These are goals within the framework of a larger, longer-term goal. You can certainly see it as one thing, but visualization requires that you break the steps required into "scenes" from your plans and how you want them to play out.

What's the outcome? For our purposes, it's the next component of visualization. Every step you've taken in the visualization process leads here. This is the realization of your goal.

Success is the outcome you desire, and you are driving the action toward that success. You're not watching a movie. You're building your reality. Putting yourself in the action as you visualize your goals and watching yourself perform the steps involved is what makes the difference between passive dreaming and active dreaming, oriented explicitly toward a successful outcome.

The detail is what your visualization should be constructed to include. Visualization even changes the way your brain works. According to Jennice Vilhaer, PhD., the more you think about something, the more it grows in prominence in your mind. It becomes more relevant to you naturally, and as it does, you gain clarity.

Let's look at an example. Maybe you're craving one of those hot dogs sold on the corner near where you work. But it's not lunchtime, and you're working. You let the hot dog go on its merry way, forgetting about it, as you have bigger fish to fry. But what if you can't?

What if you obsess about that delicious hot dog, covered in sauerkraut and mustard, or ketchup and kimchi – however you like it. What if you imagine it being slapped in a warm bun and covered in spicy, fragrant chili. Hot and juicy, you imagine its unparalleled deliciousness – a dog among dogs. You can smell that dog; you want it so badly!

If you're obsessing about that hot dog, you know you will run down to the corner, money clenched in your hungry fist. Maybe you'll eat at least 2! You visualized eating a hot dog to a level it took your cravings off the charts. It has taken on ridiculous importance in your mind, and you must quell the craving.

The lesson here is, to make your visualization come live, details matter. Those details on our hot dog example raised the craving to the level of any emergency. The realness and vibrancy of the visualization are what has driven you to the hot dog stand.

And it's that same realness and vibrancy which will press you toward your goals.

Intentionality, process, and outcome join forces to create a successful visualization, which is so finely detailed; it has become real. When it becomes real to you, you're that much closer. Using visualization is powerful. It brings your goals into focus. What's more, you're creating a permanent and abiding bond between yourself and your life's purpose. When you invest in visualization as an intentional activity, you'll enjoy substantial returns.

∾

SETTING UP FOR VISUALIZATION

The intentionality component of visualization requires that you choose a specific goal and then, plot out your visualization of satisfying it, in written form. You can think of this as a screenplay.

I always find that writing something down concretizes it. It's there in black and white. While visualizing, you'll have this at hand and, should you lose your way mid-visualization, you have your "screenplay" to take a pick at. The very act of writing down the visualization's constituent steps signals your intention and builds it.

Everyone's mind wanders, and visualization takes a certain amount of trial and error to perfect – just like every new skill. We're all familiar with those random thoughts and images that float through our minds, sometimes at surprising moments. Try not to get sidetracked by a hot dog craving! Not that you love hotdogs :).

You're directing this "movie," so don't let that hot dog on the set or into the narrative you've created. It can wait.

Once you've written down the steps in your visualization, make a list of the emotions you expect to experience once you've knocked it off your list. Emotions like happiness, joy, and pride are the most likely emotions, and you deserve to feel them because you're intentionally taking control.

The mere act of projecting your emotions enlivens your mission, getting you excited about the work that's ahead and getting it done. In visualization, you're creating deep connections with your goals. You own them, and in owning them, you're committing to them. The emotions you'll feel when the goal in question is satisfied are essential. While emotions tend to get short shrift these days, they're also where you'll discover the passion underlying your plans and purpose. And it's a passion that drives those most likely to succeed.

BREATHE INTO IT – RELAX

You've plotted out your visualization, and now, you're ready to get started. But first, let's talk about where you're going to do it.

The most important thing about your visualization space is that it's quiet and that you won't be disturbed. Of course, these conditions are very likely at 5 am, aren't they? You should be wearing comfortable clothes that don't constrict you in any way. Lay down, sit up – so long as you're comfortable with the posture you've decided on, it's all good.

Once you've settled in and you're feeling comfortable, begin by slowing your breathing down. Inhale for 5 counts and then exhale for 5.

Your body will start to relax as you breathe. If you're aware of tension in your body, address it. Lean into the tension as you breathe. Feel it relaxing. Feel blood flow through that specific part of your body while focusing on your breath.

Commit to visualization, and it becomes not only more natural, but something you're eager to do and look forward to every single day.

AFFIRMATIONS

Many write off the practice of making affirmations as "giving yourself a pep talk." While I suppose that's somewhat true, the practice goes much more profound and has a far higher value.

And yes! It's scientifically proven that affirmations have a decidedly positive impact on people who practice them regularly.

It's not "weird" to affirm your hopes and dreams. It's smart. People who have a problem saying beautiful things about themselves can gain a lot from affirmations. Not letting the world beat you down with negativity is a big part of it. You are your own best friend, and affirmations reinforce that message.

WHAT NEUROSCIENCE SAYS

Dr. Norman Doidge is a psychiatrist and researcher. In his book, The Brain That Changes Itself: Stories of Personal Triumph from the Frontier of Brain Science, he reveals the results of a study that underlines visualization's power.

The study deployed two groups of subjects. The first was asked to exercise one of their finger muscles, according to researcher specifications. The second group was only asked to visualize the exercise.

The group performing the specified exercise experienced an increase of 30% in muscle strength. The visualization group saw a 22% increase.

I think that's very impressive, especially considering that the second group didn't move a muscle – literally. All they did was visualize the exercise.

Another study I'd like to highlight here is one published in the Oxford Journal of Cognitive and Affective Neuroscience. The study confirmed that the practice of affirmations connects with areas in the brain governing reward. Researchers used functional magnetic resonance imagery (fMRI) to observe the brain's responses.

Observing these responses with fMRI support revealed that the reward centers in the brain – the ventromedial prefrontal cortex and ventral striatum- respond to pleasure – visibly increased activity, a result directly attributable to the practice of affirmations.

Affirmations were further seen to increase activity in two other parts of the brain – the posterior cingulate and medial prefrontal cortex, which both govern self-related processing.

These are the parts of the brain that respond to pain, negativity, and threat. These two areas work together as an "airbag," protecting your mental health from the distressing information your brain responds to.

This study also revealed that future-focused affirmations showed even higher activity in the brain regions we've just discussed. For example:

"I will soon be the leader in my field."

This is a future-based statement, which causes a pronounced response in the reward centers of the brain. It has a much more significant impact than, for example:

"I am becoming a leader."

When you place your affirmation in the future, you're kicking up your affirmations a notch by sending "feel good" messages to our brain's reward centers, and isn't that what we want?

Feeling good about what you're doing – being fired up and ready to achieve – is crucial to your success. Waking up every day with excitement and optimism, builds you up, and gives you the confidence to live out your purpose.

TRAIN YOUR BRAIN

An affirmation is, quite simply, a statement of fact, stated with confidence. An affirmation's role is to push you toward your purpose by realizing the goals which lead you toward it. What happens is that you are rewiring your brain to accept your confidence. While this takes time, the effect is undeniable.

We all remember running to our parents with a big idea when we were kids. We wanted to go to the moon, or maybe to another country. Or we wanted to be veterinarians or business leaders. But many of us remember the negative responses we got to our childhood dreams, often from our parents. Whoever gave us those responses, without knowing it, has made it a little more difficult for us to succeed and be truly happy in life.

This may be why so many people have difficulty with the practice of affirmations. Negative responses to our dreams and plans are just static. But we absorb them. Based on opinion and personal assumptions, there's sometimes a little wistful envy of the child reaching for the stars. Sometimes, people just want to control you, though, and keep you in your "place." It's a tall order to say positive things about yourself and your future when a rotten seed has been planted.

But you're the driver. You are in charge of your mind, so you can show all that old useless negativity the door. It's gumming up the works and slowing down the cognitive sharpness we need, to get to where we want to go.

Not believing in yourself because of what someone once said to you years ago is sad and potentially crushing. But you need confidence and courage to weed out that negativity and overcome the obstacles – which is all within you. They are not external.

Affirmations work to still that negativity and neutralize it. They heal the negativity that's nailed your feet to the floor for long enough, freeing them to move forward.

So, yes! You can train your brain, but to do it, you need the confidence that affirmations will begin to build in you.

Your brain has better things to do than to replay the dusty negativity of childhood. Affirmations are your friends on the journey, releasing you from negative thoughts and the tyranny of "you can't do that."

CREATING YOUR AFFIRMATIONS

Creating your affirmations will center you in their role. They will build your commitment to and belief in your purpose. Statements denoting action and your competencies are incredibly potent.

Keep your affirmations as positive as possible. You're training your brain to co-operate with your plans. You're rewiring it toward positivity and resilience, so filter out anything negative.

And don't forget about the future-situated affirmation as the most powerful of all. Affirmations rooted in the present will still be part of your practice. Still, future-based affirmations get you the biggest bang for your buck. Especially when you're just getting started with this new discipline, it's essential to focus on affirmations about the future, to give your brain a clear message about the direction you're moving in. Light up the brain's reward centers and watch your attitude change, and your confidence soar.

Affirmations are brief statements. They're not to belong, drawn-out essays. Try to keep your affirmations to one sentence and to keep it reasonably simple. A simple statement is much more impactful when it comes to affirmations.

As you write, be in touch with the emotions you're feeling. Many of us have lost touch with our emotions, but they're so essential to understand – they're part of you, and they're part of your success.

An affirmation that acknowledges and stirs up emotions is much more effective than one which ignores them. For example:

"I'm so proud I will achieve this goal!"

It's not only future-focused. It acknowledges your emotional landscape.

It's much more stronger than:

"I'm going to achieve this goal."

Including your emotions in affirmations allows you to name the outcome you're hoping for. You know you're going to feel something as you achieve your goals, so don't ignore that facet of what you're doing.

Something interesting about the practice of affirmation is that you're changing your brain, as you engage with them. Your brain needs to catch up to your ambition.

Some people like to look at themselves in the mirror, as they say, their affirmations. If that makes sense to you, go ahead. Everyone's different. Some don't care to do it that way. I can assure you that, mirror or no mirror, repeating your affirmations regularly, concretizes them in your mind. Your brain responds when you demand that it acknowledge a change in information with this method. You are the boss of your brain. It's there to do what you need it to do.

Affirmations don't only build up your confidence, but they build up your brain as well, making it more malleable to prompting. Write your affirmations, then say them regularly as part of your morning routine and watch all the negativity vanish.

GIVING THANKS IN ADVANCE

"The struggle ends when the gratitude begins."

— NEALE DONALD WALSH

Gratitude is tough for some. Being deeply materialistic and perhaps, narcissistic, our culture is built on the proposition of individual merit. Many of us seem to believe that everything we achieve in life is attributable to our virtues.

But many factors combine to create success. Your merit is part of it – but only part.

Gratitude acknowledges that you don't pull the levers of the universe, fate, or destiny. Sometimes things don't go your way – is that your fault, too? Rarely, I'm willing to bet.

But no one likes to blame themselves when things go wrong. Surely someone else can be blamed. But that's not how things go when you express gratitude and make it part of your lifestyle.

Genuine gratitude is transformative. It changes the way you see the world and your place in it. And in gratitude, is the genesis of unwavering personal accountability. When you're grateful, you understand the world as it is. Some live. Some die. Some achieve. Some do not. And a lot of that reality is just life's mutability.

Where personal merit comes in, humility compels gratitude. You're special. You're extraordinary. But you are not the center of the universe. Sorry.

Martin Seligman is a pioneer in psychology. Thirty years ago, he initiated the study of positive emotions, gratitude being one of them. This was extremely novel at the time, as psychologists focus had always been on negative emotions.

Seligman focused on emotions like gratitude, happiness, forgiveness, compassion, and optimism to gauge their impact on the brain.

In 2007, Robert Emmons continued the trajectory embarked on by Seligman. Emmons' work laid bare the connection gratitude has to mental health, overall life satisfaction, and life quality. Today, he is considered the world's leading expert on the psychology of gratitude.

GROWING GRATITUDE

Remember what I was telling you about in our exploration of affirmations? You learned that future-oriented affirmations were much more effective than those based on the present.

Giving thanks works much the same. That's why I highly recommend giving thanks in advance for the satisfaction of goals not yet achieved. In one of his motivational speeches at a graduation ceremony, Denzel Washington couldn't have said it any better: "Say thank you in advance for what is already yours." You're building yourself up in a completely different way, with gratitude. By expressing thanks for reaching your goals, you're also modeling humility.

And humility is one of the greatest virtues of all. It's what keeps you honest and centered in reality.

Gratitude for a positive result not yet achieved is about having faith in yourself. But it's also a humble acknowledgment that the sun does not rise and set on you alone. The sun is there for everyone, and you are no different.

Becoming accustomed to expressing your gratitude will be second nature to you before you know it. As you say, "thank you," you are admitting life is not something you control, but you'll also understand the active role you play in moving your dreams forward. Gratitude is a bridge between you and your dreams. You build the bridge brick by brick until gratitude becomes a part of you, a feature of your character.

Always express gratitude for your life's purpose and for all the goals you have in mind. That killer business idea you have is hardly more than a thought right now but say "thank you" for it anyways. Your gratitude for the idea, for the joy of creating it, and the goals you need to achieve to complete it all work together to revolutionize the way you approach life altogether. Try saying things like:

"I'm so grateful that my business idea is providing me with early retirement."

Or, *"I'm so grateful for the realization of my life's purpose."*

It's a matter of time, and you know that. But even if you don't believe in a higher power, the act of giving thanks casts you in a realistic role – that of a human who knows that life is not promised, and that effort is a type of gratitude in itself.

Now that we're in a spiritual frame of mind, let's examine mindfulness meditation as part of your morning routine.

MINDFULNESS MEDITATION

I am a fan of this practice. It's changed my life.

Remember, mindfulness meditation is a discipline. It will take some getting used to, but it's fantastic for people like us, people whose lives are purpose-driven.

But nothing in this life worth having is instantaneous. And the rewards for taking the time to explore mindfulness meditation are well worth it. I can't recommend mindfulness meditation highly enough.

I advise you to start slowly if you have not been practicing it before. It's a discipline you will master. If you've never done this style of meditation before, give yourself 5 minutes to start. Dedicate the remaining time for this item to other components of the morning routine, until you're up to speed and meditating for the full 36 minutes, each morning.

The 21st Century is a restless beast. Our minds are occupied with screens, financial worries, relationship problems, work, past failures, future fears and aspirations, all crowd to create anarchy.

Our minds zip along at the speed of light, hyperactively springing from one thought to the next. This prevents us from being where we need to be – in the present – the now.

And this is the purpose of mindfulness meditation– training you to be present in the moment.

When you live in the moment, i.e., "real-time," you're not passively taking in what's being said, what you're seeing, or what's going on around you. You are actively present. By being present, you have agreed to be a moving part of this wondrous construct of human life.

If you are a newbie to mindfulness meditation, I've provided a framework for approaching it below.

Prepare to be present in the most powerful way you ever have been.

What it Can Do

I'm sure you're all wondering what mindfulness meditation has to do with rising at 5 am. It all sounds a little spiritual!

You're a busy person. You're high-achieving and committed to living the life you want. That can get stressful. Mindfulness meditation can help with that. With this meditation style, you'll find that you're more attentive and focused and able to concentrate without difficulty. You'll also find that your emotions will be more manageable.

Here's something you'll like – your emotional intelligence, which is one of the most sought-after leadership qualities, will improve with mindfulness meditation. Empathy and respect for others are enhanced as part of this practice, and these days, these are qualities almost all organizations want to see in their leaders.

Imagine not melting down when a hitch messes up your plans or losing it because the bus is full, and you're still on the curb.

Before I started this practice, I quickly took out my frustrations on my kids when they did the slightest thing that gets me annoyed, like the toddler fighting with the 3-year-old over a toy. If you are a parent, I'm sure you can relate. Emotional regulation is also served by mindfulness meditation. By using mindfulness meditation, you'll be achieving equanimity, another critical leadership quality. This quality allows you to see both negative and positive incidents in your life as instructional, and thus of equal value. People who embrace change and failure have developed this quality in themselves, and mindfulness meditation can help you do the same.

Now, let's look at that framework!

FRAMEWORK FOR MINDFULNESS MEDITATION

With this simple framework, you'll find that mindfulness meditation comes much more easily to you.

- Choose a space you'll use every day for this purpose. Choose well, because entering your meditation space will eventually prime you for what you're about to do. This could be in your bedroom, living room, or a particular room for this purpose.
- Choose the right posture. Not everybody is comfortable in a Lotus position. If you feel that lying down makes it easier to be in the 'now,' go ahead. But you risk falling asleep, which is not what we want, don't we? My recommendation, which is what I currently practice, is sitting on a regular chair, feet flat on the floor, and sitting in an upright position. This will keep your spine straight. Gently place your hands on your thighs, turn your palms to face the roof, and close your eyes. I have found that when I close my eyes, my meditation is more effective, but it's OK to have them open as well if you choose to.
- The bottom line is, choose a technique that suits you. But also, be intentional about what's around you and how you're approaching your meditation session. Focus on your breath. Slow it down. Place items in

your meditation space that serve your practice, if possible. A candle, incense, a beautiful image – all these can help but are not a requirement at all.

- Set a timer before you begin, so it beeps at the end of the time you allotted for this part of the routine-36 minutes. Again, set a shorter timeframe and start small if you are a beginner as earlier mentioned-increments of 5 minutes.

- You are seated and ready to begin. Keep the back of your hands on your thighs, and release the tension in your arms. Be very relaxed.

- Once again, take those deep breaths, counting from 1 to 5 at a normal pace as you inhale and again as you exhale. Repeat 4 times more to get 5 rounds in total.

- Slowly return to your normal breathing rhythm and focus on it. Feel the cold air sensation through your nostrils as you inhale and the warm air sensation as you exhale. You will notice random thoughts flow into your mind. This is perfectly normal. Acknowledge those stray thoughts coming through without passing judgment or answering them with another thought. They are like passengers on the train or bus. Simply find your way to the present moment by returning your focus to your breathing.

- You might feel an itch or two on a part of your body. Try to sit with it without scratching for as long as you can-even 5 seconds. This will help enforce your ability to be patient in life and not give in to instant gratification very quickly.

- Keep on redirecting your awareness to your breathing when your mind wanders. Before you know it, 36 minutes would have gone by as peacefully as a dove soaring through the blue skies. This, my friend, is the mindful meditation phase of your morning routine.

As I said, mindfulness meditation can take a little time to master, but once you know your way to the present, you'll find that it's a source of emotional regulation, a stress, and anxiety antidote, enhanced ability to understand and empathize with other people and a defense against the useless, negative thoughts that plague your mind. It's freedom.

After 36 minutes or so of being physically motionless for the most part, it is time to get those bones and muscles moving.

EXERCISE

And now it's time to dive into everybody's favorite topic, at least mine ;) – the importance of exercise!

We all know that many people's idea of exercise is getting in and out of the recliner. Maybe that describes you! If so, grab some sweats because life's about to get a whole lot better.

At the beginning of 2020, the Mayo Clinic released a study that proved that cardiorespiratory and brain health are both improved by exercise. But the real benefit is a massive increase in grey matter and the brain, overall. This bodes well for getting older, as this effect on the brain helps fight dementia.

You're going to be healthier with regular exercise, but you're also going to have more energy, fewer mood fluctuations and a brain that will age well, so that the rest of you can, too!

Because I do not know how old you are, I'm going to talk about exercise from a demographic standpoint. Physical activity isn't just something that young people do. That said, people over 40 tend to start neglecting exercise. They get comfortable and don't understand how crucial exercise is for their ongoing health and success.

Exercise is a lifelong friend. Call on it regularly, and that friend will, in turn, grant you long life and a brain that can keep up with you on the journey.

Your 20s – hold me back!

You're an adult, and you're in your prime. All the ragged edges of adolescence are falling away, and you're as hale and hearty as you'll ever be. Start leveraging that advantage now, and you'll see dividends all through your life.

- Suppose you're already playing a sport, great! If not, find one you like and play. For people in this decade of

life, challenging exercises that are rooted in
cardiovascular exertion are ideal. Racquetball, lacrosse,
soccer – these are all excellent as ways to get your heart
rate up.

- A life cycle, a rowing machine, a road bicycle, or hiking
  and climbing are all ideal for you now. Daily exercise
  will keep your head clear and positive. Remember that
  you have 18 minutes in your morning routine to get
  this done, so using stationary equipment like the life
  cycle or rowing machine is perfect for your purpose.
  At your age, cardiovascular activity is of paramount
  importance and here's why:

People in their 20s tend to gain much more weight than they do
later in their lives. Your 20s, then, set the tone for your overall
health and wellness later in life.

The Centers for Disease Control and Prevention have gathered
data in this respect, revealing that women who weigh 150
pounds when they're 19, weigh 162 pounds just 10 years later,
at 29. The CDC's data also showed that men at 19 who weighed
175 pounds, would weigh 184 at 29.

Experts say that the best thing you can do the prevent weight
gain in your 20s is to get a scale. Weighing yourself regularly
alerts you to sudden changes. While some may have been told
it's time to watch their weight by their waistbands, the scale
doesn't lie!

And what's the best way to not gain weight? It's merely to take the time to establish the lifelong habit of exercise. And if you do gain weight in your 20s, it's much easier to get it off than it is at say, 40!

And while you're still in your 20s, learn to cook healthy meals for yourself. It's cheaper, and you know what you're eating.

But what if you don't have access to the type of equipment I've suggested? Please check out the Resources section at the end of this book for some great videos showing you time-effective, high-performance exercises for cardiovascular health, including the incredibly effective Burpee.

Now is the perfect time to commit to an exercise routine by forming a habit you'll carry with you through life. What matters most is consistency and sustainability. Don't bite off more than you can chew, but make physical activity a priority. I can't impress upon you enough the importance of establishing and honoring habits like exercise and nutritious eating as early in life as possible. The sooner you make these habits part of your lifestyle, the more likely they are to support you throughout what's going to be a fruitful, healthy life.

Your 30s – a Crucial Time

- Believe it or not, this is the decade when exercise will probably make the most profound difference to the rest of your life. Your bone density begins to decline in your 30s and your muscle mass, so weight-bearing exercises are important.

- Choose bodyweight exercises like planks, hip bridges, and pushups. Using the weight of your body is an excellent way to maintain bone density while building muscle mass. Proper form is crucial to performing a plank – especially when building to the 2-minute "gold" standard, so don't forget to check out the video on planking in the Resources section. You may even be gung-ho enough to retain a real-life expert at your local gym.

- Resistance bands are another way to build muscle and bone, making your body more impervious to injury and disease.

- Change your workouts regularly. Disciplines like Yoga and Pilates have many variations that can benefit people of all ages and add balance, grace, and stretching to what you're already doing.

Your 40s – Crunch Time

- The rubber meets the road in your 40s. If you've been active throughout your life, you'll see a remarkable difference between yourself and other members of your age group. Because it's during this decade that many people abandon physical activity and gain weight as their metabolisms have slowed down.

- If you're in your 40s and just now realizing that you need to start moving more, all is not lost. You have some catching up to do, but that's OK. You're doing something about it. Choose supportive cardiovascular exercises like fast walking, cycling, swimming, and bodyweight exercises.

- Your 40s are the doorway to middle age, so getting on the exercise bandwagon will support better overall health as you get older. Attention to your cardiovascular health is critical, as this is a dangerous decade for heart attack and stroke. As I've just mentioned above, fast walking, cycling, and swimming are excellent for cardiovascular health. At home, take a browse through the videos in the Resources section for heart helpful moves.

Your 50s – Where it Really Matters

- If the 40s are the doorway to middle age, then the 50s are the antechamber of your senior years. During this decade, if you're not exercising, you're exposing yourself to dangers like a joint failure - requiring orthopedic surgery and problems with your heart and lungs.

- Your posture begins to slip at this age if you haven't been very active. The body leans forward, as aging kicks in. You may find that your chin pokes out, and your shoulders are curving forward. To mitigate this potentiality, work on your core – this is the mid-section of your body, encompassing the abdomen, back, and glutes. When the core is strong, there's less chance of weakening your back further with bad posture.

- The plank is an exercise that can achieve tremendous things for people in their 50s. In just 2 minutes, you're working almost every muscle of your body. As I said above, watch the videos in the handy Resources section at the end of this book, or talk to a coach. The plank, when executed correctly, has an almost miraculous effect on bone and muscle density.

Your 60s – Age Gracefully

- We tend to think of this decade of life as "old age." But that perception is changing, with seniors putting many younger people to shame. Why? Because they've exercised all their lives, the importance of exercise has become more widely known.
- Because we begin having difficulty with balance at about this age, I recommend you continue with planks. The plank's focus on core muscles, while working shoulders, calves, hamstrings, and quadriceps, is the key to that.
- Lunges are another excellent exercise for this age

group. Again, these must be done correctly, so watch the video in Resources, or consult an expert.

Your 70s and beyond– Easy does it.

- Our 70s+ is the decade of slowing down. But if you've been active throughout your life, you'll be healthy while you're doing it. Your posture will be better, your muscles 4stronger, and your bone density, enviable.
- Suppose you plan to start an exercise routine at this age. In that case, I strongly advise that you consult with your doctor for recommendations or work with a movement specialist to define the parameters of possibility.

But whatever you do, don't stop moving. That's one of the worst things you can do. Even if you're a Super Senior approaching your 90s, there's still plenty you can do to help you with issues like balance and prevent muscle entropy, while maintaining good cardiovascular health. You won't want to miss the video about walking with ski poles – an excellent way to get your cardio safely as you age, keeping bones strong.

Review

Here's the part of your morning routine where you revisit those goals. Tweak them. Massage them. Don't be afraid to factor in contingencies, as we discussed earlier.

Organizing your goals with the constant reality of change in mind, fortifies them, future-proofs them, and enhances the turn-on-a-dime flexibility that gets you ahead.

Next, it's time to plan the day ahead. What's on your calendar? Meetings, appointments, picking up the kids? Just reviewing the items on your schedule gives you a sense of preparedness. Your awareness of what's coming sends you out into the world confident that you know exactly what's on your plate for the day.

Our final chapter is about moving toward your goals even faster. You're going for the gusto, so why not build your enthusiasm into select moments over the weekend?

You know you want to!

4

HOW TO ACHIEVE YOUR PURPOSE AND GOALS EVEN FASTER

As we've discussed earlier in the book, your morning routine is dedicated to your work-a-day life. But you know that while you're working, there's plenty you can be doing to achieve your purpose and goals even faster.

Learning while you work makes the time you spend making a living even more fruitful. And no, I'm not talking about sticking your nose in a book at your desk. I'm talking about latching onto opportunities to develop your aptitudes and skills. There are plenty of them all around you, and exploiting them is key to your future success.

Part of your self-development is about breaking free from accepted norms about work habits. So, let's talk about why you need to break up with multitasking for the sake of your success.

. . .

The Tyranny of Multitasking

Here's a weird fact for you – the word "multitasking" was completely unknown until it appeared in an IBM report, in 1965. The report discussed the benefits of its latest computer.

See the apparent problem? Yeah. People aren't computers. Our brains are not made of microchips. When we focus on one specific task, we're much more likely to reach mastery of the skills involved.

Lately, multitasking has increasingly been put in its place. Having been identified as the productivity-undermining claptrap it is, we are now presented with new ways of looking at how we prioritize tasks.

So, let's examine getting the tyranny of multitasking out of our lives as part of our discussion about working smarter, not harder.

More Activity, Fewer Results

Multitasking's prominence in recent decades was primarily predicated on the assumption that it made workers more productive. In fact, this assumption conflated the human brain with IBM's new computer. And while our marvelous brains are unlike computers, they are soft tissue. They're just as subject to fatigue, injury, and illness as any other part of our body. So, based on that unfortunate fact alone, the enduring presence of multitasking looming over our working lives is unwelcome.

But there are many more facts out there that will lead us to the same conclusion. Some come from a recent study by researchers at the University of North Texas and the University of Texas at Dallas.

Published in the November 2015 issue of Technology, Knowledge, and Learning, the study analyzed multitasking in a group of participants numbering 168 and implicating subjects aged 6 – 72.

While it's true that many of us have increased our ability to multitask with reasonable efficacy, thanks to electronics, outcomes don't lie. The study found that participants took longer to complete tasks which had been combined with others to assess multitasking effectiveness. In addition, accuracy was heavily impacted by combining tasks.

Bryant College's findings support this study's findings. Findings revealed that multitasking had a harmful impact on employee performance, which results in a $450 million cost per year.

The same study found that Millennials are likely to jump back and forth between online platforms 27 times in only one hour. But the brain needs time to shift gears, so our almost hyperactive multitasking costs us in the working world. It results in lower quality work, reduced creativity, crumby decision-making, and, worst of all, increased stress.

But here you are, tyrannized by multitasking. How do you break up with it? Let's take a walk through 11 strategies for giving yourself more space to focus and to avoid the tyranny of multi-tasking.

BREAKING UP WITH MULTITASKING

Follow these 11 strategies to divorce yourself from the productivity-killing habit of multitasking:

1. Stop Obsessively Checking your Phone

While this may sound counterintuitive, that's because you're used to doing it. You roll over in bed, grab your phone and check on who's seeking you out.

But making this the first thing you do each morning primes your brain to be on red alert the whole day. And while you're on red alert, you could be focusing on one important task and achieving it.

2. Get Rid of Distractions

This relates to strategy #1. To rid yourself of distractions, turn off notifications on your phone. You don't need to know about every notification because most of them – as we all know – are not a priority. Set a time to check-in and then stick to it.

3. Define the Day's Priorities

Before you get started, make a list of your priorities for the day, in order of importance. Focusing on one task at a time ensures that you do a thorough job. When you're not rushing through a series of tasks, leaping from one to the next, you're more likely to resolve them without leaving loose threads.

4. Apply Mindfulness

Here's where the mindfulness meditation you'll be practicing during your morning routine comes in handy.

Remember how we talked about dismissing random thoughts as you meditated? The same goes for your mind enumerating outstanding tasks. Dismiss them! You're working on something else, and you're going to get it done. Be present to the task you're focusing on at that moment.

5. Schedule Check-Ins

You need to check in sometimes, so schedule your check-ins. For example, check your email when you arrive at the office and at the end of the day. If you must check mid-day, do so after you return from lunch. Then, get back to the task at hand.

6. "No" is a Complete Sentence

Taking on more than is reasonably practical is a common problem for high achievers like you. But it gets in the way of doing the fantastic job you need to succeed.

People will ask you to take things on. If you have set your priorities for the day and know exactly how you plan on getting them done, saying "no" is perfectly acceptable. Politely and succinctly state why you can't honor the request. Don't go into long explanations. "No" is a complete sentence that will be understood willingly, with a simple, "I have a big day, today!". Most of your co-workers will get it.

7. Unclutter your Workspace

They say that an empty desk is a sign of someone who hasn't enough to do. I see it as a sign of a person dedicated to getting the job done.

A cluttered, chaotic desk has a psychological impact. It can make you feel overwhelmed, and that's not how you get things done. Organize your desk to be streamlined and efficient, with only those items you genuinely need on your desk.

8. Don't Procrastinate

Every high-achieving middle-class employee's life is punctuated with challenging tasks. We sometimes push them to the peripheries of our consciousness with "busy work" – also known as multitasking.

For tasks like these, put aside a little time to focus on the challenge. By wrapping your head around them before starting, you'll feel much more confident about taking them on.

9. Your Most Effective Time – the Challenging Tasks

Most of us are more effective at certain times of the day. Some find that mornings are when we're at our best. This is when you should be moving through your most challenging priorities if that describes you.

Use your "peak times" to get those daunting jobs done, scheduling the easier ones for times when you're perhaps lagging a little.

10. Journal to Identify "Peak Times"

Breaking up with multitasking gets easier when you know at what points during your working day you're most prone to falling back on it.

Having a handle on the times when you're most effective and the times when you're at your weakest is a robust tool for ridding yourself of the multitasking habit.

11. Eliminate your Social Media Habit

If you're one of the millions of people who have a problem with social media, of feeling compelled to check in every 5 minutes, there's an app for that!

Apple users can use Self Control, which is free! Cold Turkey Blocker works for both Mac and PC operating systems.

EFFICIENCY AND PRODUCTIVITY – KEYS TO SUCCESS

Multitasking kills productivity and efficiency, as we've already discussed. By breaking up with it, you'll be opening the door to a whole new world of efficiency and productivity. Producing real, measurable results is what gets you noticed and promoted!

An employee who focuses keenly on completing tasks from start to finish, leaving no stone unturned and no loose threads, is an employee who gets the promotion, the raises, and the upper management's attention. And when you're able to break up with multitasking, you'll find that you're happier, more confident, and more satisfied with your work.

By working through priority tasks, focusing on each, in turn, you're no longer in the rut of jumping from task to task, achieving little, if anything. You're achieving what the day has presented you with, and that uplifts you, your co-workers, and your supervisors. When you're a driver of office morale and success, you're a valuable asset to the company you work for.

The Cost of Multitasking

In the 1990s, two doctors, Robert Rogers and Stephen Monsell, discovered that task switching – even when predictably occurring – caused participants in the study they were conducting to be slowed down. As we switch between tasks, our brains need time to adjust themselves.

This is the executive control process, which allows us to switch between tasks. Still, the result of continually using this process over time is a loss of the ability to focus entirely.

One study showed that participants who were interrupted continuously by notifications of incoming emails scored lower on IQ testing by 10 full points. That's comparable to the reduction in IQ following a sleepless night.

So, as you can see, multitasking is a practice whose time has come and gone. Focusing keenly on one task at a time renders better results and represents a more effective way to work.

Skills Development on the Job

Any workplace that genuinely wants to benefit from its employees' potential offers opportunities for skills and knowledge upgrades. These may be everything from learning new technical skills to learning management practices toward advancement or even the C Suite.

Don't turn up your nose at what's on offer. Look beyond what your employer has on tap, too.

In a global economy, skills include languages. Do you speak, read, and write in a second language? If not, it's probably time to remedy that. If you work in a company with international offices, your employer may even be willing to invest in you by paying for a class in your chosen language. These days, that choice might be Mandarin or Cantonese, but it also might be Russian. Or it may be a language you'd never thought of learning. That language might open the door to upwardly mobile opportunities to work overseas.

Many employers actively seek out language skills and depending on your industry, there are opportunities attached, which are usually very attractive to hardworking middle-class employees like you.

Improving your computer skills is also a priority, so jump on any opportunity that crosses your desk to upgrade and enhance your knowledge. There are so many ways to upgrade; you may not be sure where to start, but mastering a second language or learning a new technologically based skill are both excellent choices.

Here's a list of what employers are rumored to be looking for, today and over the next decade:

- Superior communication skills – This remains one of the most sought-after abilities in all employment markets.
- Microsoft Office – Learning the fine points of this suite of software is crucial. That means understanding not just Word but Excel and PowerPoint.
- Detailed – Employers need to know that you see the little details in which good is found – or so they say. Having the ability to look beyond the superficial and obvious is a prized aptitude.
- Problem solver – Being able to identify problems and to devise solutions according to existing resources and information is something all employers want.

- Independent – Nobody likes to be micro-managed, but most employers don't want to micro-manage you either. It's time-consuming and annoying. They want independent-minded self-starters who aren't continually in need of support.
- People skills – Along with being a self-starter, people who can work with others as part of a team are highly prized. Having people skills may seem like a "no brainer," but employers want this soft skill for a good reason – it's not easy to find.
- Effective management of time – Employers know that time is money. Your efficiency and productivity are not just desired – they're required.
- Bilingual or multilingual – As I mentioned earlier, having a second or third language is one of the biggest draws for modern employers. Having language skills like these makes you the hottest property on the block, distinguishing you from competitors who speak only English. Mandarin and Cantonese are high on the list of preferred languages.

Other skills you might like to develop depend on the industry you work in. Perhaps, though, they relate to changes you want to make in the future. The point is to continually upgrade your skills to hone your edge in the labor market and to increase your value to your current employer.

Education isn't just something you need to do when you're young. Education is the driver of a successful life – and that's what you're focused on!

Your Evenings

You may be a single person with friends and social activities or married and needing time with your family. That's mostly what your evenings are for.

But before you hit the hay, schedule an hour to go through your goals and the skills development which accompanies them. This might take the form of reading, studying, or tweaking your goals to reflect your life purpose more fully.

What About the Weekends?

Like your evenings, you have social activities and family time to think about. Even though you're working to realize your goals and life purpose, you need social time and activities to rest, relax, and to be a whole, fully realized human being. Don't sacrifice these crucial components of a well-rounded life. It's a losing strategy.

But you need quiet time over the weekend, too. Be sure that you continue practicing mindfulness meditation, scheduling this when you can so you are your most productive. As always, I recommend the early hours of the morning because they're peaceful and it's unlikely you'll be interrupted.

You work hard already, and now, you're taking on a long-term project, so maintaining balance is extremely important. Being an absentee parent or a friend who no longer calls works against you. Keep the downtime sacred, as you can't be in self-development 24/7. It's not healthy.

But there's still a little space for you to work on your future! Making time for mindfulness meditation – about an hour a day, during a time when you'll have a little quiet, like the early morning – is something you'll be glad you did. Once you've gotten a handle on this part of your self-development journey, you'll probably find what I have – that you don't want to start the day without it!

And, while you should have one full day to attend to your personal life, that doesn't mean you can't spend some time focusing on your goals on one of either Saturday or Sunday. It's up to you how much time, but I recommend at least 30 minutes to review goals and reflect on how they're rolling out toward your purpose.

Volunteering

Volunteering is one of the most satisfying ways to network, develop, and hone your skills and to help your community while you're at it. What you may not know is that volunteering serves the volunteer as much or more than it serves the beneficiaries.

And here's a major benefit – the Stanford Social Innovation Review has described skills-based overseas volunteering as "the next executive training ground." This is at least part of the reason that such enterprises are supported financially by many corporations.

This model can certainly be applied to volunteering closer to home. In times like these, you know there are incredible opportunities out there to make a difference.

Even offering a few hours of your time a week can make a tremendous difference to organizations that have few resources to hire needed professionals in marketing, accounting, computer programming and networking, and many other areas. You'll meet people, and when you acquit yourself well, you'll make meaningful connections that can take you places.

Volunteering can even contribute to more robust health. Here are some interesting findings on that subject from VolunteerMatch:

- 29% of volunteers with chronic health conditions state that volunteering has helped them enjoy a better quality of life.
- 68% of people who had volunteered within a year of being surveyed stated that they felt physically healthier as a result.
- 89% of volunteers enjoyed an enhanced sense of wellbeing.

- 92% of volunteers said that volunteering made them feel more connected to a life purpose.

And while you're offering your expertise as a volunteer, you're building your skills and knowledge. Taking what you do for a living out of its immediate context can reveal new facets of your skillset. When you apply what you know to a need in the community, it's often true that you discover something new about yourself and your aptitudes. That can easily translate into valuable, marketable experience employers want to know about.

The New York Times and the Wall Street Journal have both published pieces which point to volunteering as a great way to find a job, too. This has happened to me. I volunteered and found one of the best jobs I'd ever had, so I'm living proof!

A survey published in the WSJ revealed that the human resources professionals participating agreed that sharing your skills in the volunteer sector made candidates for any given role stand out. Volunteering makes you much more appealing as an employment prospect.

Volunteering is a multi-faceted adventure that will undergird your stated life purpose and may even help you realize your goals along the way. And all the while, you're supporting your community, building your skills and confidence, and giving something of yourself. As Muhammad Ali once said, "Service to others is the rent you pay for your room here on earth." And, when you find the right volunteer opportunity, your service becomes a valuable part of your resume.

A SUSTAINABLE HABIT

Any habit we adopt for the right reasons must be sustainable. Habits like exercise, drinking enough water, and eating nutritiously, must only be taken up when you know you can sustainably practice them. If that's not the case, there's no way a habit will form. The same is true of changing your lifestyle to accommodate a two-hour focus on goals, purpose, centering yourself, and exercise.

Even though it only takes 21 days to form a habit, if you've bitten off more than you can chew, you'll know. And biting off more than you can chew, in this instance, usually means that you're not getting enough sleep at night. But it may also mean that you haven't approached the lifestyle change seriously enough. Let's talk about the science of forming positive habits.

21 Days to Change

You can establish any positive habit you wish to in 21 days. Whether you believe it or not, this is the truth.

So, let's talk about how to establish the habits we're talking about, especially those which comprise the morning routine you'll be following on workdays.

Resolve is not enough. Establishing lasting habits is more about consistency and self-accountability.

Dr. Maxwell Maltz is the author of Psycho-Cybernetics. Originally an audiobook, Dr. Maltz went on to sell 30 million copies of it. But this isn't where the idea that change takes 21 days to gel originates. That idea came from Dr. Maltz's plastic surgery practice.

Dr. Maltz noticed that it took a minimum of 21 days for his patients to accustom themselves to their new facial features. The mind needs time to adjust to change, and Dr. Maltz's exploration of the phenomena is the basis for a revolution in the way we think about making positive changes in our lives. The key is a consistency of practice.

The circuitry of our brains creates what are called "engrams." An excellent way to describe these is as "memory traces." The neuro-connections and pathways to do this can only be forged when we train our brains consistently for 21 days.

So, why is it so hard to establish new habits or break old ones? For starters – chemistry!

All About the Chemistry

Activation energy is the idea that a minimum amount of energy must be in place to create a chemical reaction. Only when sufficient activation energy is available can that reaction happen.

In the matter of behavioral change, you can equate activation energy to motivation. Imagine, for example, that you have a task before you're not fond of. You procrastinate. But once you get going, you feel better about what you're doing.

That means you reached activation energy's critical mass. You've stored up enough motivation to make it happen.

Several factors can act as triggers to motivate you to make changes in your life:

- A sudden realization that you need to change for pressing reasons.
- Taking incremental steps toward your goal can also be a practical way to get to that critical mass of activation energy.
- A change in the environment that increases motivation is another factor in change. If, for example, you find your motivation negatively impacted by an environmental factor – cold room in the morning – raise the temperature slightly. Or program your thermometer to "preheat" your room at around 4:30. When you rise at 5 am to start your morning routine, it'll be hospitably toasty!

Aristotle once wrote that "excellence is not an act...but a habit". And to establish that habit, a habitual, rote means must be taken to make the change stick. When done every day, without fail, a habit will be more likely to stick.

At the heart of this truth is the concept of ritual. Ritual is generally associated with religious practice, but when you think of it, we all engage in rituals. Some of us are so married to these rituals that we perform them diligently, feeling out of sorts when we're unable to.

A ritual can be anything from brushing your teeth a certain way, to feeding your pet at particular times of the day. Think about these rituals in terms of the morning routine.

The morning routine is a ritual that points you toward your life purpose.

The Power of Ritual

Clearly, the morning routine described in this book is a ritual. It's a ritual because you are actively establishing behavior that you repeat at a prescribed time, in a prescribed order, and for set periods.

There is great power in ritual, and the morning routine seeks to leverage that power, to create enhanced productivity and success in your life. The ritual itself is the desire to maintain it as a habit.

In only the last decade, scientists have shown us that the brain can be deliberately rewired. The brain is a living organism, subject to change, and ritual can help us convince it to accept new behaviors as habits. This occurs when we wrestle old behaviors to the ground in favor of new, more positively oriented ones. And it's the ritual itself which propels toward that change.

But clarity about your goals and how they're going to lead you toward fulfilling your life purpose is key to motivation – activation energy. This why the "review" section of your morning routine is crucial. Approaching your goals with fresh eyes each day ensures that you're clear about why you've set those goals and why they matter in terms of the big picture you're building with your 5 am lifestyle.

Rituals are Rational

"Human beings follow ritual practice to achieve an end. We're looking for outcomes."

In your case, you're seeking to move forward in life and to live out your purpose in a rewarding way. That is the outcome you desire from the ritual of the morning routine.

Joseph Campbell was a Professor of Literature when he began to write extensively about mythology and ritual. He wrote:

"The function of ritual...is to give form to human life, not in the way of a mere surface arrangement, but in-depth."

— JOSEPH CAMPBELL

And this is precisely the power of ritual as a rational means of creating the lives we desire. He was the person who counseled that we "follow our bliss," which is exactly what the morning routine and the 5 am lifestyle allow you to do.

Creating a ritual structure that informs each day of your work life makes the realization of your life's purpose a sacred journey. Your goals are the signposts along the way.

Rituals as a personal cornerstone, creates stability of purpose. When you're able to base what you do each day on a series of rituals, rooting your work and life in a structured sequence of actions, you're leveraging a power that the human mind has known about, without understanding it very well, for thousands of years.

And ritual is repetition. What you do each day, consistently, is what you become. With the morning routine and its spiritual, physical, intellectual, and professional aspects, you have a balanced, well-rounded launching pad to start your working day. These rituals, when repeated "religiously" – for lack of a better word – become a rational path toward your plans for a better life.

You're the Boss of You

I know you didn't come here to make excuses about being "wired" a certain way. Anyhow, you're not a robot. You have a human brain, and if there's one thing that can be said about the brain, it's that it's highly plastic – subject to reform.

Neuroplasticity is your ticket to realizing your life purpose, via your goals, and the potent rituals you'll be performing each morning on each working day. You are the boss of you, and your brain is part of that.

Despite what many believe, the brain and body are one thing. There is no separation between them. And just as your brain communicates with other parts of the body, you can deliberately convince it to change, using the 21-day formula for establishing a positive habit that will change your entire life.

Never believe, for a moment, that you're "wired" to behave a certain way. You are the electrician, and you decide what it is you need your brain to do. It's certainly not the other way around.

Thank you so much for reading. Here's to your success, with the 5 am lifestyle!

CONCLUSION

And here we are, at the end of our discussion of the rising at 5 am lifestyle. I wouldn't have written this book if I didn't know that this strategy works. It worked for me and, with consistency and commitment, it will work for you too.

This is a change that will transform your life, attitude, and work. Just by intentionally setting aside those 2 precious hours, you'll find yourself moving toward your goals – and your life purpose – in short order.

Don't be disturbed if you hit a hitch or three on your journey toward making this happen. You're as human as the rest of us, and humans, as we've discussed, don't care for change.

In undertaking the life-changing rising at 5 am a lifestyle, you're telling life that you're in charge. You're the master and commander of your life, your brain, and your purpose. While that's a lot of responsibility, you're up to it. Just remember to be kind to yourself, learn from your failures along the way, and set your alarm clock!

Again, I thank you for choosing to read this book and for seeing it through to the end. I hope you'll find it's a source of inspiration as you get rolling with the 5 am a lifestyle and all the gifts it offers to those who seek it out and practice it.

REFERENCES

Baragona, L., & Mansuroglu, A. (2019, August 29). The 11 Best Earplugs for a Good Night's Sleep. Retrieved July 13, 2020, from Men's Health website: https://www.menshealth.com/ technology-gear/g23335186/best-earplugs-for-sleeping/

Chua, C. (2009, June 9). 21 Days to Cultivate Life Transforming Habits. Retrieved July 13, 2020, from Personal Excellence website: https://personalexcellence.co/blog/21-day-trial/

Dulin, D. (2019, August 26). The Incredible Power of Visualizing Your Goals. Retrieved July 13, 2020, from Unfinished Success website: https://www.unfinishedsuccess.com/the-importance-of-visualizing-your-goals/

Kamen, R. (2015, April 1). The Transformative Power Of Gratitude. Retrieved July 13, 2020, from HuffPost website: https://

www.huffpost.com/entry/the-transformative-power-_2_b_6982152?guccounter=2

Kissel, K. (2010, January 19). How to Practice Mindfulness Meditation. Retrieved from Psychology Today website: https://www.psychologytoday.com/us/blog/the-courage-be-present/201001/how-practice-mindfulness-meditation

Macdonald, B. (2017, September 6). How To Use A Planner To Organize Your Life In 4 Steps. Retrieved July 13, 2020, from Career Girl Daily website: https://www.careergirldaily.com/use-planner-organize-life/

Manson, M. (2014, September 18). 7 Strange Questions That Help You Find Your Life Purpose. Retrieved from Mark Manson website: https://markmanson.net/life-purpose

Moore, K. (2020, April 29). Positive Daily Affirmations: Is There Science Behind It? Retrieved from PositivePsychology.com website: https://positivepsychology.com/daily-affirmations/

Riopel, L. (2019, June 14). The Importance, Benefits, and Value of Goal Setting. Retrieved from PositivePsychology.com website: https://positivepsychology.com/benefits-goal-setting/

Sports and Exercise at Every Age. (2018, April 20). Retrieved from familydoctor.org website: https://familydoctor.org/sports-and-exercise-at-every-age/

Why You Should Wake Up Early Every Morning, According to Science. (2018, November 2). Retrieved July 13, 2020, from Power of Positivity: Positive Thinking & Attitude website: https://www.powerofpositivity.com/why-you-should-wake-up-early/

RESOURCES

I've included exercise videos to ensure you're doing the exercises described in this book correctly. I've also included two links to well-known online volunteering hubs.

EXERCISE

Burpees are a full body exercise which implicates cardiovascular systems, while enhancing explosive strength in the lower body.

Planks are one of the most effective body weight exercises ever. See how to execute a plank correctly, in this video.

Lunges are an excellent way to maintain lower body strength and balance. Learn how with this instructional video.

Chair Yoga is an excellent practice for people in their 70s and 80s, or those who have balance issues to build up their muscles.

Nordic Ski Walking is an superior means of retaining cardio-vascular health, balance and muscle strength.

VOLUNTEERING

Catchafire matches your expertise with volunteer opportunities. An excellent and acknowledged resource.

Linkedin 4Good creates better communities using a network of volunteers.

www.ingramcontent.com/pod-product-compliance
Lightning Source LLC
Chambersburg PA
CBHW020421130626
46549CB00006B/2671